THE SOCIAL WORLD

JEM AMBER STONE

Hi. Let me introduce myself and some brief information to why I'm re-publishing this book. I was born in 196? in England. As of present (2022) I am widowed and live alone with my little dog Zahara on the Sunshine Coast Qld. Australia. I am many things: mother, grand-mother, singer, writer, psychic/medium, and I collect dolls, dragons, gothic stuff, and rocks. I possess many post-graduate degrees mainly obtained from the University of New England in Armidale NSW. I have spent 50 years plus studying with the last 2020 when my husband tragically died. This was followed by my beloved 9 y.o. dog Jimmy dying last year. I have suffered a lot of trauma in my life; starting with the survival of an abusive, toxic, dysfunctional childhood. I am the author of many books. Xlibris originally in social published the listed: Of the Of Seeing the spirituality behind the negativity - a menu for the game of life. The second ed. Of both these are now through Kindle/Amazon as are the other books I have authored including: Sing the song of bards. His name was Jimmy and he was my special dog; Coming clean - Remember Rob; and the Balance. Please look forward to another book soon to come titled 'The Maurs'.

The reason for re-publishing two of my books, including this one, is because despite spending thousands of dollars with the company to get published, and despite sales I have not received one cent for MY work. I should have read the fine print - I'm not a citizen of the US. Now xlibris will claim they have paid me royalties, but my bank records clearly show I've received nil. Yet I get letters from their parent company showing me sales and taxes. Kindle is now my preferred choice because there is no outlay of fee until book is sold then one pays printing costs and can receive 40 – 60% royalty. I am very angry that a company has profited (Xlibris) from my work. They did not write those books. I did and so I believe I'm entitled to receiving something if a book is sold.

The last and important reason for re-publishing the Social World is because in my naivety I presented it originally as a serious study of sociology. It could be as it is my theories, but perhaps it may be more general or metaphysical. Please enjoy!

C 2022 J. A. Stone

Sociology I view as similar to psychology: theories! Psychology is the study of an individual, and more specifically thoughts, sub-conscious, behaviour, acts, reactions taking into account nature and nuture. Now you will hear Sociologists getting very upset if one starts to delve into the Psychology realm, but here is my counter-argument. An individual is an unit of society and therefore what makes that person 'tick' impacts on interactions in society and influences structures of society. So for me the two go hand in hand, and I can hear my lecturers grasping for air and saying "no wonder you only just passed sociology!" (It was one of my majors in my BA. Interesting I achieved distinctions and higher when it came to psychology.) I want to make it very clear Sociology is NOT a science as it is interpretative, prejudiced, biased, and fallible. By what mathematical rules can be applied to it? Even science, itself, are nothing more than theories.

CONTENTS

INTRODUCTION

BASIC QUESTIONS THE SOCIOLOGY STUDENT
SHOULD ASK:

1.\ Is the social world independent of its' actors?
2.\ Do children have a sense of social order?
3.\ At what age do we develop this sense?
4.\ Are we born with no idea, or concept of social order?
5.\ Deviancy? Is this 'true consciousness' as the critical theorist Habermas describes?
6.\ Subjective meaning? Limitations? No actor has the same – what I feel, think, see – another person cannot feel the same as me.

WHERE DOES SOCIOLOGY START?

Sociologists generally concentrate on one of the following or all as a whole:

•\ Functions of society.
•\ Functions of institutions.
•\ Functions of units of society.
•\ The individual or social member. (Although some sociologists argue this is psychology.)
•\ Language and communication.
•\ Social action.

•\   Rules and norms.
•\   Social situations.   Etc.

I decided to write this book because whilst I was studying for my Bachelor of Arts in the 1980's, of which then sociology and education were my majors, I became aware of problems, I and fellow students faced in dealing with the subject of sociology. I guess that each one of us started with our own particular brand of sociological theory, and believed it to be just as 'right' as Max Weber, or Garfunkel, or Blumer, and why not? Marxism, Structural Functionalism, you name it, can they really disprove the many other theories that abound about sociology? Maybe each one has only shown part of the overall schema of things, or maybe we just haven't yet discovered the truth, and so sociological research continues. Maybe there is no right answer.

I state this because no matter what other theorists view, our world is made up of us. We are a collective term for you, me, and all other individuals that exist on this planet. This book is not written as a direct critique of other theories. I can relate to the many and varied concepts. Take for example: Phenomethodology: stepping outside to comprehend; or Critical Theory: the notion of false consciousness. Freud can also be useful! This book was intended for the sociology student to also question the science of sociology itself. A book, I highly recommend is titled "What is this thing called Science", by Chalmers.

My last point before the book proper: is the fact psychology and sociology going to great lengths to be different. But are they? Isn't Freud a sociologist too? Did he not try to analyse why an individual behaved in a certain way? Isn't behaviour a social (re)action? My view is that both strains of behavioural sciences focus on the unit known as the individual. Okay: so macro sociology focuses on society as a whole, but, how can they go past people? People who are the creators or builders of society, social institutions, practices, and so forth. Macro sociology should not ignore the existence of the individual. Other sociologists look at the human social actions. Again, I would argue that this delves into the psychology realm: or are we just mindless robots, empty vessels? What about our motives, irrational behaviours, deviancy, etc.?

Anyway: please enjoy my book on a sociological theory that was originally written 1987. Note at end of chapter 17 Terminology, are three questions I might be asked. I have labelled this my appendix.

CHAPTER 1

WHAT IS SOCIOLOGY?

Good question. As a student, I often wondered if some of the sociological theories were really just philosophy. Sociologists view sociology as a science thus the name social science. Generally sociology can be divided into macro sociology, and micro sociology.

Basically, macro sociology looks at the whole, or how different parts of society function, how they operate in the macro sense. They do not take into account individual, psychological make-up, or genetics, or nurturing. For example, they would study the structure of a school, how it works, its' functions (to educate), and how this institution relates or interacts with other parts of society. This is my crude definition. One of these would be Structural Functionalism.

Micro sociology on the other hand concerns itself with humans or social actors, their social behaviours, their practices, their languages, rules, norms, social order, social structure and so forth. Some of these perspectives are Symbolic Interactionism, and Ethnomethodology.

Therefore, sociology focuses on humans, their behaviours, practices, interactions, belief systems, culture, language, social structure, and society as a whole, etc. Now one can observe measure, read other books look at history, research, statistics, and arrive at some sort of sociological conclusion, which are some of the methods used in the so-called science of sociology. Clarifying: some sociology relies on quantative, verifiable data, while others use interpretations as their methods to arrive at sociological theories. It all depends on the view

1

point. Some theories try to place sociology as a natural science, which follows natural laws. Thus the social world is 'out there' and exists without us. This is known as empiricism, and positivism, and is held by such theories as Structural Functionalism, which measures and verifies data. Others such as Symbolic Interactionism believe that we as social agents construct social reality. They criticize the theories that believe sociology is a natural science. Instead they concentrate on the social actors and how social actors perceive and construct the social world, and by what methods, etc. Usually, then, this sociological view interprets.

There are many books on the subject of sociology and many that define and explain the different theories. It isn't my purpose to do such. I have only offered an extremely broad and crude generalization of the science of sociology, so that the reader has some basic awareness of the existence of the major theories that are used and taught at university level. However it is my contention that not one of the many theories used are completely right, and in fact, I would criticize some of them, that they have sociology very, very wrong. If there was a right theory, why would poor, suffering sociological students at university still have to study all the different sociological theories and perspectives? It is because they all have serious limitations! Equally though: it is not my intention to state my theory is right or better or more plausible. Yours could be just as right, or wrong.

So: what is sociology? I now assert sociology is not a science. Science has rules, logic, axioms, etc. It would be okay to nominate sociology as a science if the study of society could be proven to be rational and logical. The argument then arises that the very building blocks of society, which is ourselves, is far from rational, even though the structures we have made seem to have a rational and fulfilling purpose. Maths, astronomy, physics, chemistry all does follow laws. Two plus two also equals four. We can prove or disprove scientific theories by the application of natural laws and logical reasoning. Those that believe sociology as a science: that it follows some natural laws are fooling themselves because of the very nature of humans who have created the social world. Natural law cannot explain human chaos, or rebellion, or upheaval, or deviancy, or mental illness, or religious belief. Perhaps it can explain natural language since we have rules for it, like grammar, the way words are pronounced etc.

No two people are alike. We differ genetically, biologically, in our personalities, and in our upbringing. We have different beliefs, ethics, morals, and viewpoints. Our 'social class status' varies, as does our race and culture. Economic and political forces affect us. We are educated differently. We learn differently, through different senses, and at our own pace, and level of understanding. Some of us are good at sport. Some of us are deviants, criminals, or 'mentally ill'. Some of us are creative, dreamers, whilst others are intellectual, rational, and some are business orientated. We are individuals with our own individual make-up nurtured individually. Everyone can think, talk, act, behave, dream, react, or interact with each other and the societal world in some way even if it's a form of deviant behaviour.

Biologists have studied bees, and have found that once a bee has located a potential source of pollen, the bee dances in a certain way to let other bees know where it is. Sociologists have not proven that in a given situation you and I will act in the same way: like for example every bee does. Humans seem to be unique. So to believe sociology is a science is to neglect or ignore free will.

Free will is important. Some philosophers believe we possess free will, while others argue its' validity. I would argue free will does exist. However, we do not, off course, have free will to be born. That is very much dependent on other factors. Once born, we can put up with our chosen life of our own free will, or we can rebel. You may argue free will does not exist because society forces us to accept and its' rules or we are punished. Consequences do exist. Like Newton found: for every action there is an equal and opposite reaction. However, imagine if a large group decided of their own free will not to conform to the society they live in. Sometimes there is a consequence of show of force from the ruling government, but, at other times there is chaos, war, and even change. Sometimes an individual who refuses to accept is ostracized and forced to find his/her niche elsewhere. Society is formed by joint free will consensus.

Sociology, then, is basically the study of us: social animals. More specifically, the social individual and his/her behaviour in society. This does not mean we cannot study society as a whole, or in parts. We have built these parts for a meaningful purpose. For example: a school to educate. Therefore sociology can study the functions, purposes, rules, roles, and practices of these units of society, and apply this to a broader picture. As an individual we also play many different parts or roles: mother; wife; sister; daughter; friend; worker; and so on. Hence as micro sociology we could study these parts to understand their necessity.

Equally important to understand: is that every one of us observes the social world, and has a sociological theory. We are constantly interpreting, and analysing our own behavioural patterns, and that of others. We do so to understand the social world we live in, to make sense of ourselves, and to legitimate our own selves in it. Our perceptions also differ. Our senses lie. From our common perceptions, and views, arises generalizations, and stereotyping. These, themselves, make interesting sociological theories.

Furthermore, sociology is biased because it is based on the sociologist's own make-up, perceptions, senses, and interpretations. Even statistics are open to biases. Empirical data is not infallible. Sociology cannot be measured or compared. Statistics can only tell you how many people on such a day did such and such: i.e. it is only a numerical value, and does not give explanations of why, or of motives. Thus sociologists that use these methods and then come up with a 'proven' theory are only theorizing their own interpretations of what they perceived on that day. They have not necessarily explained why people practise 'a', or the motivation behind why people go to institute 'b'. For a better approach to the problem, each individual when they did 'a' or went to 'b' would have to be intensively studied to ascertain their reasoning, and interactions behind it, and then the researcher would end up with thousands of dis-similar theories because that may only be applicable on that particular day. The next day or in the future their reasons etc. may change.

The last point about 'what is sociology' is that one cannot distinguish between sociology and psychology. To arrive at an acceptable sociological theory about us as social being, and our creations: social structures: we need to look at the mind, the psyche, the ego, the 'id'. We need to accept that sociologists themselves are a creation of society.

CHAPTER 2

THE SOCIAL WORLD

Does society or the social world exist out there as an independent entity? The answer is NO. Throughout history, we have had different forms of society, and as social individuals have created each one.

As soon as we are born, we are born into a role, and upon acceptance of this role, we begin to behave in a certain way as dictated by that role. We are given gender: boy/girl. We are given objects such as toys to further our acceptance. Non-acceptance is known as deviancy, and once we deviate away from the norm, our creation for us is destroyed. It is no use insisting you are a girl if biological and genetical factors say otherwise (a rule): so the male gender is now given other roles: son, brother, father etc. If this boy still exists he is a girl, then often others will view him as not normal, and therefore for this individual the social role and gender of boy no longer exists. That creation has broken down.

Our social world with all its' structures, rules, norms, and so on exists because we created it and as a creation we accept it and believe it has an independent existence. Without some form of social structure we would not exist as unique social beings. We made rules to stop chaos. Roles are created so we can partake and interact in the social world. If there was no social order as such we would not need language, for what would be the use of communication? We would exist independently, and thus cease to be social beings.

In the case of bees, if the bee did not dance in the right way, no other bee would be able to locate the pollen, and so social interaction has broken down. The bee is no longer interacting with the other bees.

We may hate society, resent its' power, and say it's repressive, capitalist, materialistic, or whatever, but, we are the ones who structured our social world as such. We are born into these structures and usually consensually we all accept it and so it continues to be. When there is massive non-acceptance, and populations uprise, and revolts follow, the old structures are often torn down, and new ones reformed, and we accept these new ones until they either no longer serve their purpose, or we no longer believe in their validity in our lives. When there is individual non-acceptance and rebellion, that individual is ostracized by the other accepting members who label the non-conformist as a deviant. This deviant then becomes a hermit, or a criminal, or mentally ill, or substance user, or eccentric etc. Rarely, some deviant is seen as enlightened and they become charismatic leaders of new uprisings, heroes, cult leaders, politicians, artists etc. Acceptance of social structure continues its' existence. We are programmed to accept (usually).

Now we come to the notion of 'free will'. We do have choices, but, right from an early age, we come to the realization that no matter how many faults there are inherent in our system, our world, we have to put up with them if we wish to survive, and be accepted by our peers, and significant others. From the time we are born we are being 'socialized'. We are taught language, how to behave, and so on. These processes maintain our society. Through them, we begin to believe in and accept our social world, its' constructs, and its' structures. We do have free will. We can choose the patch our lives will follow. We cannot choose our gender, family, social class, race that we are born into (although there are some religious belief systems that uphold that we do indeed freely choose these things to experience life).

However after birth, societal forces and pressures begin to act upon us repressing our free will, teaching us that to survive we must act or behave as society dictates. Usually, we do not fight these forces, but, rather willingly accept them. Our growing up is controlled and structured. Our own language is one of the societal forces, and through the use of language, we arrive at the point where objects are given names, descriptions, meanings, and attributes, and values are also placed upon them, and how important they are in society, which overall means how valuable they are to us. Our belief in their worth sustains their existence.

We are responsible for everything as we created it all including our social world with our collective free will. For society to undergo change would mean rethinking, and we would no longer believe that the present social world and all its' components had any significant meaning for us. We would then reconstruct a new one and give it new attributes.

We have children, and by our own practices, and beliefs, which make up our social world, we 'force' our descendants into believing and accepting the world out there, which we created: that it really is real, and exists independently of the creators, ourselves. We have unconsciously and deliberately as a whole blinded ourselves to the fact the social world is not permanent, but, very much dependent on our continuous belief in its' existence. Hence we have close our minds to truths, buried our free will, and like mechanical, programmed robots continue to construct our creation: the social world.

In fact, those sociologists who insist in the reality of a social world add to the confusion. They also ensure that through their beliefs the social world is a valid, independent, and very real entity. There are also authorities we have set up to make sure we keep on believing in the validity of the social world. This we have reasoned is for our own good.

CHAPTER 3

THE INDIVIDUAL

The individual is the agent who constructs, and builds the different social units, which make up the social world. This individual clothes him/herself with certain attributes to use in the role(s) s/he acts out in the game of life. If we view life as a game, things become clearer. In any game there are participants, rules, goals, and objectives. Society is a type of game we play. We start at the beginning (birth), where we are given our gender, and from there, we choose paths to follow. We are rewarded for right choices and punished for mistakes.

One individual interacts with another and this is called a relationship. These relationships can be brief, permanent (lasting a life-time), impersonal, or intimate, and are also used in the building of social structure. One such structure or unit is the family. We are born into this family, thus there can be parents, children, and siblings. This relationship we often view as personal, intimate and permanent (I will always have a mother: etc.). Yet we have created this unit. This unit has a meaning for us, thus, the family in the social world continues to survive and exist.

The individual is the basic building block of the fabric of society. When several basic blocks are cemented together, we have a family. Other units in society are work units, which make up businesses, employment, cash flow, etc.; students in class in schools or other educational units; and so on. Each of these units is comprised of individuals whom have, by consensus, attached a name to the unit, as well as function, meaning,

8

and value. The members have created the unit, and have even created rules to how the unit functions, and by being an active part of the unit have made the unit a 'living, functioning' structure of society.

The individual is born with consciousness, and with a mind that has to grasp and understand the symbols of the world, interpret these symbols of the world into which they have been born into. Language is a useful tool for learning. Through the use of words, thoughts, and ideas, the individual begins to make sense of the social world. The individual learns to understand and be understood.

When two individuals engage in a personal relationship, emotions come into play and bonds are formed. These personal relationships can also be negative as in enmity, and war. The emotions felt in the relationship and even after the relationships end, adds validity to the meaning of relationships, and aid in the construction of society.

Example: Husband and wife: two individuals whom have decided to relate to each other in a deep meaningful way. Once, however, love has gone, then the validity and meaning of husband and wife for those individuals and a social unit (marriage) has broken down.

So, emotions and feelings are part of the social act or game that give relationships and the worth of oneself: validity; significance; and meaning. Through these basic social units, the individual as a single entity finds him/herself, their place in society, and gives meaning, and purpose to their game of life. These units seem to be necessary not only to construct our social world, but, vital to our continued existence as an individual. For if this was not the case, we would not be bothered to socially interact. The existence of the social world gives us validity of our own existence and necessity of life.

CHAPTER 4

PSYCHE/SELF

It is the inner reality of the self that gives us our thoughts, motives, and emotions. In this inner reality we interpret the social world and behave accordingly. The inner reality can be broadly divided into two levels: conscious and sub-conscious. In the conscious state, there are thought processes, which affect our behaviours and interactions. In the sub-conscious state, we dream, and possibly our underlying motives, feelings, and emotions arise here. This is the place where we conceive of constructs to what is real.

Below diagram of I = self I

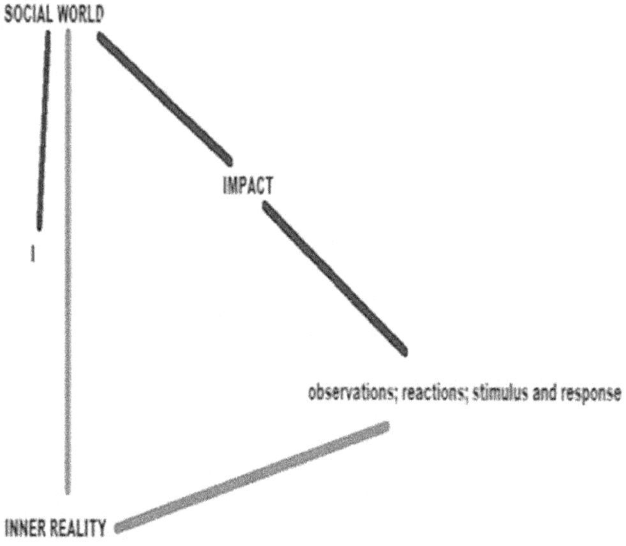

Self is not the physical body, and is not one's thoughts, and is not one's feelings. Self is all of these. Self is the 'whom' or entity that is behind all these levels. Self is whom who feels, and whom who dreams, and whom who reacts, and whom who constructs reality.

Society does influence self. It is the part of self, which accepts its' role in society and decides to behave in or not in acceptable ways. Society does not completely control or possess this entity or self, otherwise we would not think, and we would not be able to rebel, and collectively revolt.

Thus the self is composed of many facets, and presents a different one to the outside in different circumstances, different roles, and at different times. The self learns and matures and grows. Therefore the question must be asked: what is true self?

CHAPTER 5

DEVELOPMENT

Many psychologists, and sociologists, believe that for us to be functioning units in society that we must go through many stages of development. Each stage 'matures' us. If this is so why do we act at times so childishly in adulthood? Often as adults, we are expected to act in acceptable ways, but, sometimes we do not. Why is it: that as children we seemed to be free, has no stress, and deal and plays with fantasy, and overall be honest with what is really out there? Adulthood brings stress, anxiety, deviancy, stunted growth problems, and general dysfunction. We also become more apt at lies.

In many of our intimate relationships, we have problems, because we have lost our sense of self, and innocence we experienced in childhood. It is probable that this loss of self in adulthood had allowed us to continue in the creation of the game of society. As children, we seem to be able to perceive things much clearer often playing games of pretence. Yet these games can reflect the roles we will take on as adults. As we are educated, programmed, and pass through these so-called developmental stages, for which the purpose is to become functional social beings, we are actually, in my belief, taking steps backwards into the fantasy land. Irrational behaviour seems to be formed in the very early stages of maturation. These stages never leave us, and are present all the time in our lives: some of them locked forever deep down in our psyche. The older we become, the more we learn what society expects of us, and so many of us learn to hide the immature early stages.

12

CHAPTER 6

PURPOSES OR FUNCTIONS OF STRUCTURES IN SOCIETY

Firstly let us revise. In this book, it has been stated social units are made up of individuals or members. It was also suggested that we created these social units, and by attaching meaning, value, attributes, names, purposes, etc., that this continues the unit's existence in our social world. Furthermore, even when we find fault with a specific unit, it can still exist if it has meaning for society as a whole. One a unit has become nominal, the members then form rules by which the unit functions. Members are expected to behave in certain ways and relate to each other in some way because of this unit. This unit has been formed to serve a purpose, or for some function.

Let us examine for example what seems to be a permanent structure or unit: the school. School was created so children could be educated. All it really is: is a heap of buildings. They have no power or value by themselves, so, to make school more real, we invented classes, pupils, and teachers. We then went further into our creation and invented uniforms. School students wearing uniforms somehow made the creation more powerful and gave it meaning. There are also rules that have to be obeyed at school as well as time tables. Now: what happens when a child rebels against school? In their mind, perhaps education and schooling does not have the meaning and significance it does for the other 'positive' acceptors and creators (other children, educators, parents etc.). Remember too: when a child is growing up we encourage

13

and socialize the child into believing in the reality of schools, their usefulness, their importance in one's life, their significance to self-worth. "You will not obtain a good job unless you get a good education and do well!" For the one who is the rebel, school ceases to exist. Sure: the teachers, the buildings, etc., are still there, but, the validity has gone.

Another important point to make about all units is although consensus and common belief set them up: this does not necessarily mean every member holds the same attitudes or beliefs about the unit. There are individual differences to just exactly what the unit means. This also impacts on how much the member becomes involved in the unit. Examples: P. and C. at the school, or a president of some club etc.: whilst other members are quite happy to be passive. The fact we believe this unit has some purpose or meaning in our society is enough to for it to exist 'independently' of how one views it; whether negative or positive. By this it is meant that an individual can view a unit in a negative light and still the unit functions. Criminals and police are a classic example of opposite view points and of a structure, or unit.

Since these units form the structure of our social world, we need to validate them, and thus rules are created forcing us to act in certain ways. Laws and law enforcers come into being. Again: this gives our creation more substance and validity and more reality, and ensures the social structures' ongoing existence. We then take on roles to act out parts for the different structures, which give meaning to the social world.

We make the structures or units more real by the use of raw materials such as buildings, clothing, etc. We give value to these raw materials. Money has buying and spending power and other properties that are not actually inherent in the money itself, but, in its' perceived image, and importance to social members. Each raw material serves a purpose in our creation and in the game of life. So: cars, houses, possessions etc., are the hard substances, real objects that seemingly are able to be perceived by our senses or our outer reality to give the creation its' existence and validity. But: can we trust our senses? These objects are tools or stage props that players use in the game of social play. Now because the use of materials is to build the 'settings' or stage of the creation: this makes things seem real: i.e. that the social world does exist out there independent of us: its' actors. Our personal possessions describe our individual roles, give it attributes, and further contribute to the so-called reality of social structures and society. We do not realize that the validity of the social world only exists in inner reality: our own psyche.

This is necessary, I feel, i.e. the notion of 'false consciousness'. To believe in the world, to partake seriously in it, we have to forget the inner reality where we constructed what is out there. We have also created certain symbols of the social world, which is interpreted in the inner reality or psyche, for the purpose of further hiding in our false consciousness, so out there can continue to be. The social world is very much dependent on the false consciousness of the collective mindset of social actors or game players.

CHAPTER 7

POWER OF MONEY

Western, and modernised societies are structured around money. To be able to survive in these societies, money is necessary. We work for money, use money, to buy food, clothing, shelter, entertainment, etc. Money pays the bills, and buys luxuries. In fact, the more money you have, it seems the more importance, power, and esteem from others, you also inherit. Most people would aspire to be rich. Money seems that necessary and possesses such magical qualities that criminals steal it and even kill to own a large quantity.

But: what actually is money? The raw materials are often paper, copper, or some other metal, or alloys. Does this in this form already have a given value? No! Money only becomes money after being stamped with some form of label, and when we believe in its' power: its' spending and buying powers. Money only becomes money and of any worth after certain attributes has been added to the raw material. We could have chosen leaves and nominated them as money. Money allows a society to barter, buy, sell, trade, and bargain.

'The love of money is a necessary evil' is quite a famous proverb. Money and crime are well linked and researched. The so-called sickness in our society could also be linked to money or more accurately, to greed. The proverb makes a good sociological theory worthy of further investigation!

From the concept of power of money, classes in society are formed, such as a capitalist society etc. (For a more thorough treatise on classes,

16

and class structure, consult a book that deals with the subject. Marxism is one such topic.) The divisions in society are a direct consequence of the power of money.

The power of money is sustained because of our belief in its' power and value. For example, if a man threw away a lot of fifty dollar bills, we would label him 'mad' because we would think what a waste of money seeing it is such a lot of money to just idly throw away. Money has great value in our eyes, for if it did not, we would be throwing money away too like that man, seeing them as useless pieces of paper. In fact that is all those fifty dollar bills are: paper: where some authority like money banks (another unit or structure we created) have printed fifty dollars on them, and voile they are now worth fifty dollars!

Money, then, is a vital, basic unit of our society, and is created by us, and its' existence is sustained by us in our belief in its' independent reality. As soon as these material objects no longer have meaning or significance for us, they then cease to exist, and the structures of the social world begins to crumble.

Therefore one area of sociology could concentrate or focus on the symbolic meaning of money and its' relationship to the social agents (us). The point can be illustrated by the following example: Mrs. B is a housewife, mother, and is employed on a casual basis. She clothes herself, lives in a house, drives a car, earns and spends money. Each of these things has meaning for her. She believes in their solidity and uses that to project an image she can relate and make sense of. She uses these tools to survive and participate in society. If she suddenly stopped doing the normal things of her everyday life, they would have no longer any meaning or value for her. Thus: for her, they would cease to exist.

Money is only money because we nominated it as such, and gave it the necessary attributes of money. In conclusion, therefore, money and other impersonal/personal objects have now become subject to our personal meanings and have been given attributes and values on which we have based our society. Our beliefs have created and sustained their existence.

CHAPTER 8

RELIGION

Why is religion necessary? Is it to find truth behind the falseness of creations? Or: to find a way out of the deceptions, corruptions of our creations? To find true meaning? To find inner reality? To find perfection? To find enlightenment?

What about those who claim to believe in nothing? Do they? They obviously believe in the validity of the social world, and in their own existence (in it).

Religion, basically, is a set of beliefs. I would claim that belief in our social world and its' structures could be interpreted as religious. The love of money or worldly goods becomes a type of worship with those objects becoming idols or gods.

Sociology also studies religion because this practice (s) has its' own set of rules and is part of the structure of society. Religion provides valuable insights in cross cultural belief systems. Religion has also created another layer: that of the spiritual realm.

Some of us would argue that they do not believe in their own existence as if they were part of a higher being's imagination, or computer program, or that everything is just a delusion, or a mass hallucination, or matrix. I am a great admirer of the philosopher Descartes who believed, "I think, therefore I am………"

The mere fact these sceptics and disbelievers feel, act, behave, participate in the social world shows that in some way they exist. Society exists from our own creativity. Maybe, we are part of that creativity

18

too. We gave the entity of the social world 'life' so are we not ourselves living entities, even if that is created too? For me, scepticism, cynicism, disbelief in existence or in God is just another belief system or religion. From our beliefs, we construct our own reality and our own god. Perhaps sociology itself could also be interpreted as religion. I would almost definitely label psychology (especially Freud and other analysts) as a type of religious belief.

Christianity, one religion, teaches healing of soul, body, heart, and mind. Christianity has left a huge impact on many western societies with its rules, and as at time throughout history been the governing body, the authority, telling us how to construct the society we wanted to live in. To this day many religions in different countries still dictate how one must live. Psychology analyses and tries to heal the mind. In both Christianity and psychology there must be acceptance of self. Sociology differs (advocates argue) because it is not a study of the mind: but: isn't the social world a creation our of collective consciousness and unconsciousness of social actors? In other words created from our own minds. Can not the ills of society be cured by the treatment of the psyche?

Religion, therefore, must be held responsible for also allowing social actors to perceive the social world as real. The church, history reveals, dictated good, moral behaviour, and provided laws for citizens to abide by. Many of our wars have been holy wars: often to convert or subdue heathens as their society and practices were not acceptable, or appropriate in the eyes of the powerful church. Witches were burned and horribly tortured because they were not acceptable in society. Seemingly, they had strange powers and deviated from the norm. So if a babe sickened and died, an old hag, for example was blamed.

Religions need money to build places of worship thus creating another social structure and giving more power and meaning to objects such as money, buildings, holy objects etc. Religion was also a consultant in marriage. Once, birth, marriage, and death were all registered in the church records.

The ten commandments of the Old Testament have become part of our laws enforced by law agents such as:

1.\ Thou shalt not steal.
2.\ Thou shalt not commit murder.

Others like:

1.\ Thou shalt not commit adultery.
2.\ Honour your father and mother:

Have become the norms of our western society, and considered to be morals, ethics, but not enforced laws punished or enforced by law agencies. Punishment for these may include ostracization by others.

Likewise, in non-Christian societies, people are ruled by religious beliefs. ("Things fall apart" is a fiction book, which deals with an African Tribe based on reality. Here the tribe never ventured out at night because evil spirits walked.)

So: practices and rules of society are very much governed by belief systems. Religion impacts on our thinking and our behaviour, and thus, has a direct effect on the creation and maintenance of social worlds. Religion over human history has run and controlled social actors and their social worlds, and because of the power, which has been invested in it, has at times been corrupt, evil, and able to be corrupted. Yet the social actors themselves are responsible for the creation of all religion.

A famous Persian emperor had conquered the Ancient Greek World, and had burned Athens, but because the gods were unfavourable, he quickly returned back to his known land. This shows us the influence of religion even on our governing bodies.

CHAPTER 9

MENTAL ILLNESS

Mental illness is described by others as abnormal thinking, and/or abnormal behaviour. It may be self-induced as from drugs, or it may be faulty brain mechanisms, chemical imbalance: maybe: as a result of 'bad' nurturing, or genetical, or whatever reason. Mental illness is regarded as deviancy, and means that an 'abnormal' mind is dealing with society or vice-versa. When mental illness becomes a serious problem, the patient/or criminal is instutionalized as s/he is perceived as a danger to themselves, or to others, or society.

The 'abnormal' mind can no longer be programmed into socializing. These people are seen to be living in unreality. (Yet what about our geniuses, and our charismatic leaders.)

I would theorize to believe in a social world's real existence is living in unreality and the perhaps the 'mentally ill' are ourselves: acceptable, passive social beings. Who knows: perhaps the perceived 'mentally ill' actually perceive real reality? For them: society and its' associated functions and meanings have lost their value, significance, and reality.

MENTAL ILLNESS IS JUST A LABEL

Some religions view mental illness as demon induced. They believe the cause to be spiritual. Thus spiritual beings (evil) have thrown a spanner in the works of programming the individual into being an acceptable member of society. Since religion is seeking enlightenment and focusing on the spiritual realm (since that is the belief where we all go after death), why then are exorcisms used, and prayer for the lost soul (mentally ill)? Doesn't the mentally ill person perceive the social world as not real thanks to the assistance of the spiritual world (if indeed demons exist in that level)? Simply put: religious people also view the social world as real and that demons 'screw' up the structures and behaviours of human beings. Maybe it is society that is the real 'demon'.

Many people who have been brought up in dysfunctional families, (abusive, alcoholic, etc.), suffer problems, and experience crises in adult life, and many are labelled mentally ill. To adjust and become normal, therapy is often sought. Therefore it is this dysfunction in our nurturing that has roots in our adult dysfunction. This shows the importance of a functioning family unit in today's society. It shows that the programming and education begins in childhood.

CHAPTER 10

METHODS OF HOW
SOCIETY IS RUN

Simplistically society is run on power and control. (For abuse and corruption please consult that chapter.)

There are many levels of power structures in society from basic to complicated. Usually by consensus power is given to this structure to control and govern the social world.

At the very basic level, we have control and power over ourselves. We can control our inner reality by stimulus and response: this in turn governs our participation in the social world and our perceptions. When we become involved in a relationship power and control can become unequal. The more complicated and larger a relationship becomes: the more probability unequal power exists. Then power struggles come into play. In personal relationships, we are often able do something about this, but, in more complicated, impersonal relationships, there is nothing we can do, unless many dissatisfied members decide to uprise and revolt. Often we have built a structure to have power and control over us to safeguard our creation. The police make sure we act as law abiding citizens.

Examples of control and power mechanisms:

- \ Teachers control students.
- \ Parents control children.

                    Jem Amber Stone

•\   Money controls our lives, and living standards.
•\   Banks control money.

Other factors outside our social creation can also exert power and influence over us: things such as weather, climate, disasters, and so on.

CHAPTER 11

CHEMICAL ABUSE AND SUICIDE

Like religion where god is in control over lives and events, chemicals can be used as a crutch to survive the social world. Chemicals can be an escape route. Certain chemicals, it has been stated, show alternative realities. Authorities ban many chemical substances, and especially the ones that show a different 'world', whether true, or hallucination.

Suicide is also about control. The suicidee has perceived s/he can finally choose whether they wish to live in society or not. It no longer holds a value for them. Suicide and chemical abuse exist because the structures of society become not real, or far too real, (see below diagram).

Re

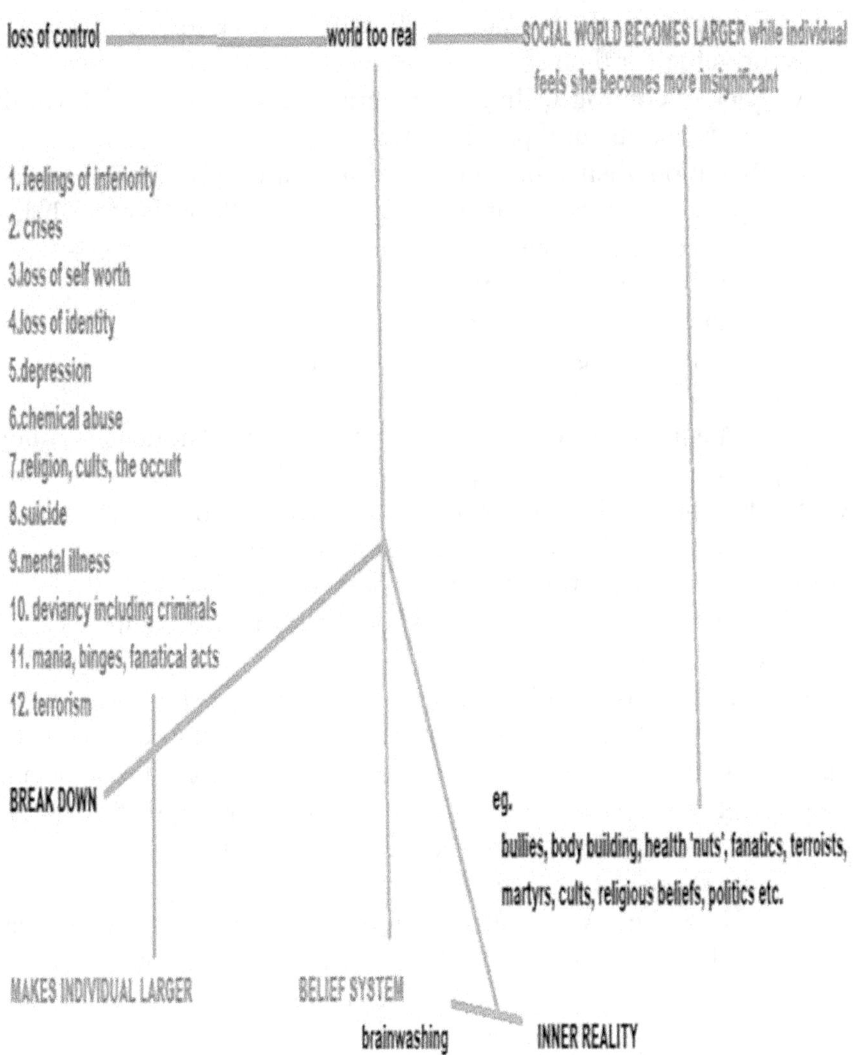

loss of control
world too real
SOCIAL WORLD BECOMES LARGER while individual feels s/he becomes more insignificant
1. feelings of inferiority
2. crises
3.loss of self worth
4.loss of identity
5.depression
6.chemical abuse
7.religion, cults, the occult
8.suicide
9.mental illness
10. deviancy including criminals
11. mania, binges, fanatical acts
12. terrorism
BREAK DOWN
eg.
bullies, body building, health 'nuts', fanatics, terroists, martyrs, cults, religious beliefs, politics etc.
MAKES INDIVIDUAL LARGER
BELIEF SYSTEM
brainwashing
INNER REALITY

REASONS FOR DRUG/ALCOHOL, CHEMICAL ABUSE etc.

- •\ Like in a religion search for a real reality.
- •\ Social world unable to satisfy.
- •\ Method of control – they can choose their own reality.
- •\ Dysfunctional: nurturing problems; mental problems; deviancy: not acting in the normal way because normal has no meaning or value for them.
- •\ Lack of control: feeling of powerlessness in a powerful world; life is chaotic and problematic.
- •\ Rebellion: dislike of society and structures; problems; labelled a 'rebel', accepts the label and takes on the attributes of a label; just because one can.
- •\ Leisure and enjoyment.
- •\ Medicine e.g. Pain management.
- •\ Unable to cope with the social world.

Often the alternative reality of example being 'stoned' is much more pleasurable than living straight in the social world, and eventually, chemical dependency occurs. Chemicals are continued to be used/ abused despite the risks, which suggest there are serious concerns with this reality we have built.

What happens to an individual when their sense of control is lost? Crises, lowering of self-esteem, and feelings of powerlessness, are but the tip of the iceberg. Life's events take on enormous proportions and impact on the sufferer's life so that s/he feels that these things or the situation controls the actions and behaviour. That is: these events have the power to elicit the individual's reactions rather than the individual choosing to react in a certain way: (maybe we can't). They feel loss of choice and decision making.

This is cyclic. A situation could arise where in reality an individual does not have control: (for example in a court of law): and thus, has these feelings because a more powerful agent has forced its' control and decisions on the individual's life, such as a judge's ruling and sentencing of a criminal. Adverse situations can therefore affect individual feelings of self-control.

CHAPTER 12

CORRUPTION

Corruption is an abuse of power, and/or control, and/or resources. Society is run by individuals who have usually been elected, or by force taken government, and these individuals are in positions of power. They have control over our economics of our money based society. They bring down governing laws.

Greed and power are often the motives for corruption. In a money-orientated world, and a desire for material wealth, has created an abuse of privileges given to governments, financial institutions, police, and other structures. Sometimes it is a matter of a religious belief that causes the abuse. Corruption occurs at all levels, but, the higher up one is in society, and the more power one wields, the more likely one is to get away with it.

Even with our law enforcers, corruption is rife. There have been many instances of police bribery and brutality. Even in courts of law, it does not count for honesty, but, rather who is more believed even if they are lying. Once again, an abuse of privileges given to these structures or units of society.

The very nature of human beings is open to corruption. All types of societies have these problems. The world we created is imperfect because of the flaws of human nature.

Control starts at birth. There are many dysfunctional families, where one person has abused their power and trust. The family is a very simple unit of the social world. Where abuse has occurred, the child often grows up feeling like a victim, powerless, lacking self-esteem, or out of control.

Sometimes, and very often, more complex organizations will also abuse their power. Wherever there is inequality there is oppression, and the consequences are crime, deviancy, mental illness, apathy, suicide, and revolts.

CHAPTER 13

DEATH

For all of us, we desire to know what happens after death. Death is a natural event in our lives, which can happen suddenly, tragically, or at the end of a very long life. When death nears, and at this stage of life, the social world and reality start to lose their meaning, and qualities. For some this has already occurred with diseases like dementia etc. We may feel frightened of dying because death means the unknown, and all we have known is the reality of socialized human beings. For some: death is the solution. For others: death is just the next phase; and for others: death means being with God, or back to real reality. Nobody has actually died, then woken up after a very long period, and told us exactly what does exist. There are off course: NDE's where people have 'died' and reported on tunnels, spirit guides, deceased relatives, god, bright lights, hell, and so on.

The brain is a strange organ. It can hallucinate and believe that the experience is real reality, and it can create an outer reality that it believes exists independently. Our brains interpret symbols and give meaning to the reality of the physical world: but: who is to say this is real? When the brain 'dies' there is no longer the means to process and interpret data. Nothing would have meaning. This physical reality, a construct, ceases to exist.

30

For me, death means the end of being a social being, and whether there exists new planes, or realities, where we live/inhabit is unknown and unknowable. Maybe there are spiritual sociologists studying real reality there! I believe that whatever 'we' are continues on in some new form, or new way, or maybe, we get to do this all over again.

CHAPTER 14

THEORIES AND THEORY CONSTRUCTION

What is a theory? This is a really hard definition for there are theories about that. In sociology, you will often find the term inter-changeable with approach, or perspective, or view. These are misleading for they don't give a clear meaning. Very simply, a theory is a set of ideas (yet to be proven) that is put together about a certain thing. A theory contains one or more assumptions. Theories can be tested and proved to be true or not, although, some sociological theories cannot be tested. An example is Phenomethodology because these sociologists believe that no two situations are the same, and no two interpretations would perceive a given situation as the same.

Should sociological theory be testable? That depends on your viewpoint. I would tend to side with Phenomethodology. It would be hard to test because of the individualistic nature involved in research. No two individuals are the same, and our motives are different. We may act in similar ways, but, reasons behind it may differ. They may not. We all may be wired to act to accept society: except for deviants, and mentally ill. Also: given the same set of circumstances, an individual may act completely different. All we can do is make generalizations. The use of statistics has too many variables to prove something one hundred percent.

Does this mean sociology should then revert back to armchair philosophy? No: not necessarily. No matter how small an interaction

32

is, it is still worthy of study because this increases our knowledge of the social world. All experience is worthy of research: all acts: behaviour: language: social structure: etc. because each piece fits the giant jigsaw puzzle, which make up the social world, our complicated, multi-layered creation.

How do we construct theories? We construct our own theories all the time. We are constantly analysing, assuming things about our environment. Each of us has our own concepts of what makes our society tick. So: how do we construct plausible theories?

Sometimes, I wonder how certain psychologists and sociologists have derived at their theories. Piaget for example just observed his own three children, and then became famous, with Piagetian schools set up. How are some of their theories plausible? Some of them have caused great amusement. What is important is: that all theories result in useful insights and also makes us re-examine our own ideas. If some-one provides a plausible theory then it could become another sociological theory providing us with some information, and also one where other sociologists must study, prove, or disprove, criticize, or agree. Not all of our knowledge is right or justifiable. We are learning all the time. Sociologists are not infallible and thus theories are prone to error.

When science boomed in our past, a lot of scepticism arose. In what do we believe? This is an healthy attitude. To question and doubt all theories is a way of arriving perhaps at true knowledge, and at real reality.

CHAPTER 15

MORE THOUGHTS

I believe money was created for another purpose: one, which is not obvious, but, intrinsic. Money was created to add power to those in control: to give financial institutions, and those in control of wealth: more power over social members.

For example: the average person takes a loan from a bank to buy a house. The bank creates this money or loan. In reality, the money is just a figure. This mortgage rules the life of the individual. S/he now has a debt. Interestingly, the bank does not actually create real money to cover interest on loans thus the world economy is always in debit as it naturally follows that there is not enough money to go around to pay off the added interest. Money in banks can just be a figure on their computers. Therefore the more there are loans (the more that is owed), the more power and control the rich and the government have over the ordinary citizen. Banks are allowed by governments to create money, but only so much money is made.

This particular creation is a major factor in the inequalities that exist in society. These will continue to exist as long as social members continue to accept the conditions under which creation like money exists.

ON RELIGION

Just one simple thought. In times of terrible disasters, world castrophes, etc. even the disbeliever, the sceptic turns to God. Sometimes, at first, God is blamed and anger directed there. Why did God let this happen? Or: there is prayer offered: "please God don't let this happen!" Often people who see evil in the social creation turn to God in the hope that the creators of the social world will be cleansed from 'sin'. Their hopes in a heaven are a hope in a perfect creation.

ON CREATION

A creation only reflects the characteristics of its' creator/s, and is created for a purpose. When the creator finds it repulsive, then it is destroyed. It only takes the power of one to show the faults. By unity, can a creation be made, as one can be made in enmity in this game of life.

CHAPTER 16

FORBIDDEN FRUIT OF KNOWLEDGE

(This chapter looks at meanings and interpretations loosely based on the Ancient Greek philosophers Aristotle, and Plato.) I have also used Newton's third law of physics.

In previous chapters, emotions and inner reality, and how we interpret the social world was discussed. How can we feel or react (social behaviour) unless there is an equal and opposite feeling or reaction. This is as close as we can come to a logical formula except the qualities and quantities that make up those logical/rational formulae are themselves emotionally based, and any psychologist could argue that emotions are irrational. An interesting side-track would be to compare instinct and the emotions we as social beings all feel. Are emotions a programmed reaction to socializing? Do all cultures feel similar emotions in certain social situations?

So: how do we not only react, but, also judge? By judge, I mean set/create/dismantle the basic moral standards. These starting points or building material create for us meaningful partnerships: family, school, employment, etc. Where do these building blocks come from? Are we born with them? Christians believe so given a doctrine of the forbidden fruit of knowledge.

It does not matter how primitive a civilization seems to be. For every action there is reaction. For every feeling there is an opposite feeling. For every value/quality there is an opposite. This is the oriental yin/ yang principle, and our human live are very much dictated by them.

36

Below are examples:

POSITIVE ATTRIBUTES	OPPOSITE/NEGATIVE
Good	Bad
Beautiful	Ugly
Right	Wrong
Honest	Lies
White	Black (this is not negative)
Female	Male (this is not negative)
Hot	Cold (this is also not negative)
Christian	Demon

We cannot appreciate the attributes of something, including a social structure without understanding its' opposite. If everything was exactly the same, we would not be aware of opposites, but, in our social world no two structures should they be 'solid' like a building, or relationships, is the same. How can we compare or put a value on our social world if we do not have opposites.

For example: if every object was exactly the same level of beauty, with exactly the same amount of goodness, we would have no realization of ugliness, and furthermore, we would not even understand what beauty or goodness was.

If we had no sense of right and wrong, there would be no need for laws: (here is where forbidden fruit comes into the equation)! If there was no love, no need for emotional partnerships, marriages would not be necessary, and perhaps, as a consequence, our reproduction of our species would be in jeopardy. Young would be left to fend for themselves. Nurturing and love would not exist. Likewise it there was no love, there would be no opposites, and this could imply the dying out of the human race. Interestingly having no opposite of love has a good consequence: for there would be no wars.

So: if all our values and social structures is favourable, society continues to exist in its' present form. We can only change when we become aware of opposites and that our values are negative.

The last point in this chapter is this: it is one for you to investigate as a sociological, or psychological, or philosophical student. Why do we fear and act negatively to negative qualities and assume that beautiful things are inherently good? Satan is supposed to be beautiful. Perhaps it is that if we knew beautiful and evil could go hand in hand would create chaos in our inner psyche and change forever our reality.

CHAPTER 17

TERMINOLOGY

(Please note that these are my terms. My past sociology lecturers may/ not agree with them.) These are not in alphabetical order.

SCIENCE: Knowledge that is testable, and has rules, and theories derived and constructed from natural laws. These rules follow the physical universe.

SOCIOLOGY: Interpretation of people's behaviours, as well as analysis of society and structure. It looks at practices, language, culture, classes, etc. From observations of both micro and macro, 'building' blocks of society, theories are constructed, but, because of biases, prejudices, and personal interpretations, these theories cannot be tested (unlike mathematical equations which can be). Sociology is the study of the creators (us) and our creation: the social world or society.

SOCIETY (SOCIAL WORLD): An entity entirely dependent on its' creators. It was created and constructed from the collective consciousness of our inner realities.

ACTORS: We, the creators, when we take on our roles in the game of life.

COLLECTIVE CONSCIOUSNESS: Everybody's or the masses of individuals' psyches.

DEVIANCY: Most of sociology views deviancy as not conforming to the norm. In my view, deviant behaviour and thoughts, occurs when an individual no longer believes in the validity or reality of a certain thing in the social world. The norms of society have no significance or meaning for them.

CULTURE: The meaningful practices of the different peoples that populate earth. What has validity for one culture is meaningless in another. Culture is a set of practices that enable society to function, and continue to exist, and gives meaning for players.

LANGUAGE: This is divided into many levels. In inner reality: symbols, signs of the outer world are analysed and interpreted. Language is basically a means of communication.

There is the spoken language. This is where oral words used have meaning by which players are able to communicate and form bonds that give relationships meaning, and construct our society. The words make objects real. By giving the objects a name and attributes we have given our world meaning.

Language and words differ in different cultures for the purpose of attaching meaning, constructing reality, and socializing, through communication. Without language in some form there would be no socialization and breakdown of society would occur.

Language is probably the only construct that has rules. The way it is spoken and written. There is spelling and grammar and punctuation: all follow rules. These differ in different countries.

MONEY: An object made by us from raw materials, which has been assigned a value and meaning, and used in exchange of goods and services. Goods are objects either luxuries or necessities used in our lives. Services are provided by employees, businesses, etc. Our society is very much based on a buy/sell/trade relationship. However if it was a 'free for all' money or the need for money would probably not exist.

ROLE: Examples: mother, father, employer, shopkeeper, governor etc. Roles are parts, social players, take on when acting in the creative play/drama of the social world. They define our place in society, giving us identities, and nominating our functions in society.

RULES: Rules dictate how games are played. In society, rules tell an individual how to act, how to portray their role, and boundaries of acceptable behaviour.

Example: Game of Education

Teacher\ educates/passes on knowledge, has authority, control,
      and power.
Students\ listens, absorbs, learns, behaves.

In the above game, there exists its' own rules and roles: separate from other games. A student has set rules on how to behave as a student. These rules differ when s/he goes home and becomes the child (son/ daughter, brother/sister) for then it comes the game of family and what is allowed in the game of education many not be enforced or allowed in the game of family.

Rules may be clear, concise, and legally enforced. For example in the game of 'let's play shop', there are necessary roles to play of consumer (buyer) and seller. As the buyer goods are bought and paid for. Now if I decided I wanted to change the rules and not play the game properly there would be severe consequence and penalties if I decided to steal. Maybe, the significance of paying for my goods has no meaning for me. As I am deviating from the norm there are then forces brought into play to punish me for my actions, and to correct my inappropriate behaviour. I'm caught stealing and I am arrested by the law enforcers, the police.

So: there are rules that been concreted into laws, and enforced by law agents.

Children learn rules of the games of life at an early age. This can be found in their play when they are imitating the grown up social world. Examples are mummies and daddies; doctors and nurses; school etc. Often a child will explore the avenues by opting to be 'bad' in these games. For example a naughty school student. This reinforces appropriate behaviour, and teaches children rules of the game.

Rules have been set so we are forced to act in certain ways, and to maintain social practices. Rules arose from consensus. From them, other social structures developed (police, court system etc.) to enforce the laws so everyone will behave in the way society has dictated. We do not want or desire deviancy, rebellion, for such actions undoes the very fabric of the social world and invites chaos. Human beings seem to need rules to know how to play as social actors.

Rules can also be vague, blurred, and limited. Rules can be 'understood' (collective consciousness). Example would be that picking your nose in public is not really acceptable. Now if you deviate are you arrested by a law enforcer? These types of rules called morals and ethics are more subtle and arise from learned behaviours. The child is taught these acceptable social behaviours.

After birth, we must learn the rules to be able to exist, and survive in our creation. Rules are part of programming the individual to be a member of society, and to make sure society continues to be, and to give meaning to social games.

As already discussed language has rules, but there are subtle ones too. Certain tones of voice indicate emotional state. Language is a process, which involves listening and talking (conveying meaning across/communicating), i.e. receiving and giving. Two people cannot talk at the same time otherwise they are not communicating. Words, symbols, signs, have been given consensual meaning understood by all. The listener not only interprets what the speaker says into meaningful symbols, but, knows intuitively what the speaker is referring to, unless, of course, s/he was speaking in a different language to what the listener knew.

GAMES: As individuals or as a collection of individuals in society, we seem to be unware that society is just a game, and within this game, many smaller games are being played.

It is a game of make-believe, a more sophisticated version of our childhood: fantasies where society, its' structures, and rules, exist out there independently of its members. We do not know it is pretend as that memory was buried so all will behave as acceptable social beings. If we arrived at the knowledge that life was a game, we would lose our socialisation, for society and its' components would no longer have serious meaning or power over us.

We play every day. We play being men/women, husband/wife, teacher/pupil, criminal/police officer etc. We can even play the game of deviancy.

PROGRAMMING: Processes which occur from birth onwards, of socialization, and accepting the social world exists.

CORRUPTION: This occurs when individuals who have control abuse it.

APPENDIX

SOME QUESTIONS

1.\ Do children have a sense of social order?

Children are taught. You are not born with the ability to eat, talk, etc., you are taught!

2.\ Are we born with no idea or concept of social order?

Right. At birth we are innocent.

Some authorities would disagree arguing that some of attitudes are inherited, that they are present in our genes. These specialists tested some young children and concluded some of the so-called male chauvinistic attitudes can be found in young boys during play, and not from what their parents have taught them. These judgments are once again: biased and open to interpretation. It is my opinion that the behaviour exhibited by these young children was learned, even perhaps from watching television.

A baby is only concerned with its' own needs: hunger, pain etc. Until the baby grows older there is no interest in social interactions. We learn attitudes through different types of experience and sensory inputs.

43

3.\ What is the real reality you refer to?

Some seek enlightenment, others hallucinate with drugs, to find this. I do believe in a spiritual realm. Obviously we will not really know until death has claimed us.

Physical objects can be felt and perceived. Our senses tell us that they are there. They seem real. Are they? We could argue the point and perhaps arrive at conclusions similar to Descartes.

Real reality is perhaps a spiritual issue. When we die our reality for us now (the creation, the social world), ceases to exist and have meaning for us.

Therefore sociology can only deal with what is real for us now. So: if we are functioning in normal, acceptable ways then the social world becomes our real reality. Perhaps we have lost our sense that once knew it for what it was: a creation and a game. Before all of this and throughout history, it appears societies have become more complex, but, once we knew real reality. In order to survive and cope in our modern day, technological society, we have lost this knowledge. We have blinded ourselves. Real reality is locked inside of us, deep in the inner layers of inner reality, and while we continue to play or act out in the social world, we will remain blind. This is necessary for our creation to exist. Thus real reality becomes a dream or non-existent. This is why we are always searching for that elusive something.

www.ingramcontent.com/pod-product-compliance
Lightning Source LLC
Chambersburg PA
CBHW081539250726
48659CB00009B/3007